731
P

13830

Pountney, Kate

Make a mobile

DATE			
DEC. 18.1981			
DEC 20 85			
JAN 6 '86			

Make a Mobile

Kate Pountney

S. G. PHILLIPS ✗ NEW YORK

731
P

Library of Congress Cataloging in Publication Data

SUMMARY: Instructions for making progressively more
difficult mobiles including moving toys, simple mobiles,
and balanced mobiles.
1.   Mobiles (Sculpture)—Juvenile literature.
[1.   Mobiles (Sculpture)]   I.   Title.
TT 910.P68   731'.55   74-9824
ISBN 0-87599-206-4

Library of Congress Catalog Card Number: 74-9824

ISBN: 87599-206-4

Printed in Great Britain.
First U.S. Edition.
S. G. PHILLIPS, INC.

Contents

TABLE OF EQUIVALENT TERMS

British Terms	American Equivalents
Set Square	Right triangle
19 S.W.G. or 1 mm. wire	Narrow gauge piano wire or fine spool wire found in hardware stores
UHU, Bostic	Page's Glue or similar all purpose clear adhesive
Card	Oak tag or cardboard
Sellotape	Scotch tape or other cellophane tape
Greaseproof paper	Wax paper
Turps substitute	Turpentine substitute
Convector heater	Electric heater
Garden cane	Thin bamboo cane
Fire	Heater
Cotton reels	Sewing thread spools

Introduction

The word 'mobile' means moving, so a mobile is any object you can make which will be constantly in motion. It can be something pretty like a flight of coloured paper butterflies suspended from the ceiling and floating gently in a draught, or funny like a clown bouncing from a spring with waving arms and legs, or useful such as a weather vane in the garden swinging round with the wind. The exciting thing about mobiles is that once you've made them they spring into a life of their own. They swirl and twist, and move about in strange and unexpected ways, so that you will get as much fun and interest out of watching the completed mobile as you will from making it.

The first mobiles in this book are simple to make, and then more skill is gradually required as new principles and techniques are described. So, when you first start, it is best to work from the front through to the back of the book rather than attempting one of the more complicated constructions straight away. Always read the instructions carefully, then assemble all the materials and tools required. Try to work in a clear space on a table or in the corner of a room, so that you can see exactly what you are doing. In this way you are less likely to get into a muddle. Never be impatient and rush through the instructions to achieve a quick result, because this nearly always results in a badly made object which you won't feel happy about. Instead work carefully and always wait for any glue or paint to dry before going on to the next stage. If you do have any difficulties don't forget you can always ask your parents or a teacher for some help: they are probably longing for any good excuse to try making some of these mobiles themselves!

Mobile making is fascinating because it combines so many different skills and talents. Whether your favourite subject is art and you enjoy creating things full of colour and pattern, or whether you prefer scientific subjects, learning how to make things work, and experimenting with new ideas, there will be lots of things to interest you in this book.

Tools and Materials

The tools and materials required to start making mobiles are very simple and inexpensive, and you will probably already have most of them at home. The *Basic Equipment* list below is what you really cannot do without. Anything else should be bought as and when it is required.

Basic Equipment
Pencil
Ruler
Scissors
Sharp knife (e.g. penknife)
Compass
Set Square or square corner of
   cardboard

Equipment for work with wire or wood
Small saw
Hammer
Pair of pliers with a wire cutting
   attachment
Coil of wire—wire comes in different
   thicknesses called standard wire
   gauge (S.W.G.) or in millimetres
   (mm.). 19 S.W.G. or 1 mm. wire
   is a suitable thickness for most
   mobile constructions.

ADHESIVES
All purpose clear adhesive   This is a quick setting adhesive which will stick just about everything from cardboard to glass. It usually comes in tubes and is available under a variety of brand names (UHU, Bostic, etc.) in most hardware and general stores.

Sellotape or Scotch tape   This is very useful for all sorts of general sticking jobs. Available in most stores and shops.

PAPER AND CARD
Card   Comes in a variety of colours and thicknesses. For most mobile work choose a smooth white card which can easily be cut with scissors. Buy it from artists' materials shops, an art and craft department in a large store or some stationery and toyshops. An empty cardboard box cut into pieces will often work just as well as a sheet of card.

Paper   As well as using ordinary white drawing paper, try experimenting with all the different coloured and patterned papers you can buy. Decorative wrapping paper, rolls of coloured cellophane, shiny silver tin foil, packets of coloured tissue paper and crêpe paper are all available from stationers' shops and large stores.

Tracing Paper   Available at artists' materials shops, some stationers' shops and large stores. Greaseproof paper, normally used for wrapping food, will work just as well and is usually cheaper to buy. Ask your mother if she has some in the kitchen.

THREADS AND STRINGS

They come in a wide variety of thickness and strength. Available in many shops and general stores. Transparent nylon thread is particularly good for suspending mobiles because it is almost invisible and very strong. Available at model-making shops and some general stores. To suspend light objects made from card or paper, ordinary black or white sewing cotton works very well.

WOOD

Have a good look round your local woodwork or model-making shop. They often have small cheap offcuts of wood that are very useful for mobile making.

Balsa wood   This comes in thin sheets, blocks and sticks. It is very light and so soft that it can be cut with a sharp knife. It is a particularly good material to use if you have not done much woodwork, but remember that it is not very strong.

PAINTS

To paint on paper   Use any water-based paint such as water colours from a paint box, finger paints, powder paints, tubes of gouache, tubes or small jars of poster paint.

To paint on wood   Water-based paints will work but they will soak into the grain of the wood and rub off easily. For a more permanent and better effect use a small tin of gloss or matt household paint. Available from large stores and hardware shops.

To paint on wire or metal   Use enamel paints. Tiny tins or bottles are available in model-making shops, art and crafts shops, some toyshops and general stores.

   If you use a gloss or enamel paint you will need a bottle of turps-substitute to clean your brush afterwards. Available from hardware stores, household and paint departments of large stores.

DECORATIONS

How you decorate your mobiles is of course entirely up to you. Here are a few things you can buy or collect that might come in useful:

   Coloured felt-tip pens, patterned and coloured Sellotape, packets of gummed paper shapes, sheets of stick-on stars or spots, 'stick-on glitter' kits, tinsel Christmas decorations. All available from large stores and stationers' shops.

   Tear out and keep the pages from old comics and magazines which have nice colours and patterns. They will be very useful for stick-on collage decoration. Start a collection of corks, small, interestingly shaped plastic and cardboard cartons and containers, scraps of material, braid, wool and ribbon, you never know, one day they might be just what you want!

Windmill

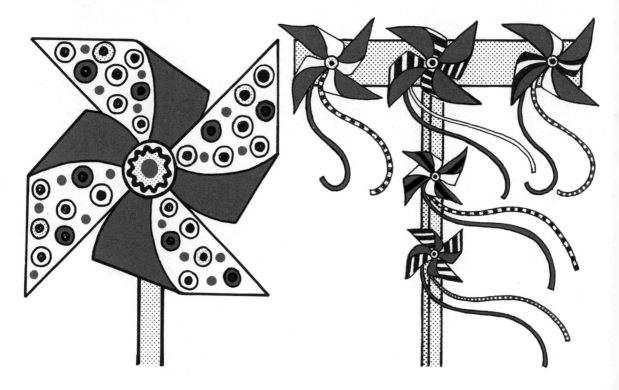

Materials	Tools
Stiff paper	Pencil
Cork	Ruler
Slim wooden stick	Set square
Pin	Scissors
Two small beads that will thread easily onto the pin and not slip over the pin head	Knife
	Compass
All-purpose clear adhesive	
Paints or crayons	

Windmill Stick Cut the stick to any length you like, sharpen one end to a point and push it into the side of a cork (fig. 1). If necessary make a hole in the cork first with a sharp metal point.

Windmill Cut out a 6 in. (15 cm.) square of stiff paper and join each pair of opposite corners with a diagonal line. The point where the two lines cross is the centre of the square. With your compass draw a circle from this centre point, radius $1\frac{1}{2}$ in. (4 cm.). Cut along the diagonal lines from each corner to the edge of the circle.

·8

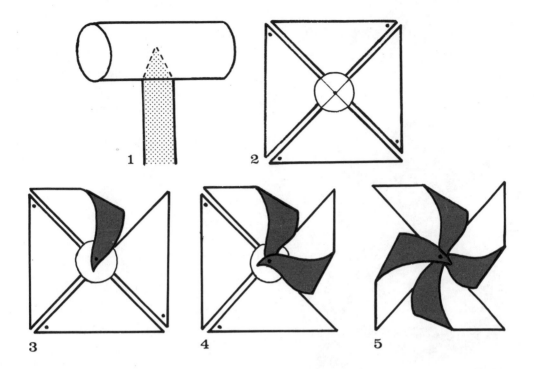

Decorate both sides of the square with paint, crayons, or coloured gummed paper. Bold simple patterns will look the most effective because when the windmill is going round, the colours will blur into each other.

With a pin, pierce a small hole at the centre point and four alternate corners of the square (fig. 2). Bend each pierced corner to the centre (figs. 3, 4, 5) until the windmill shape is completed. Place one bead on the pin and stick the pin through all the pierced holes to the back of the windmill, then thread the other bead onto the pin. Push the pin firmly into the soft cork at the point of the stick.

VARIATIONS

Multiple windmill stick   The drawing on the opposite page shows a stick which holds several windmills. A strip of thick card or wood is placed across the top of a square ended stick to form a T shape, and the two are lashed together with strong thread. Several corks are glued to the structure with all-purpose clear adhesive, and a windmill attached to each one. Be sure to leave plenty of space between each cork so that the windmills can move freely.

Huge windmill   This is made from a very large square of card—the bigger the better! Decorate with bold bright colours, and tie to a tree or garden fence.

Windmill flowers   Make three or four windmills, paint the sticks green and glue on some large green paper leaves. Push the bottom of the sticks firmly into a plant pot full of earth, and you will have an amusing arrangement of flowers.

Spiral Mobile

Materials
Thin card
Stiff paper
Tracing paper
Cork from a bottle
All-purpose clear adhesive
Darning needle
Paints or crayons

Tools
Pencil
Scissors

Draw or trace the spiral onto thin card and cut round the outline. Then cut along the red spiral line round and round to the centre. Draw or trace the figure onto stiff paper and cut it out.

Paint a face, hair, arms and the top of a dress on the figure. She should have a back view on one side and a front view on the other side. Decorate the spiral so that it will look like a skirt.

To attach the figure to the spiral, fold the tab at the bottom of the figure along the dotted line and stick it in the position shown at the centre of the spiral.

To make a base for the mobile, stick the sharp end of the needle into the cork so that it stands upright. Make a small dent with a pin in the centre bottom of the spiral and then carefully balance it on the blunt tip of the needle. The needle must not go through the spiral.

Place the mobile above a hot air current, for example over a radiator or a convector heater. Hot air currents in a room always rise upwards, and the force of the continuous current will make the figure spin round and round as though she is dancing.

If the spiral is floppy and hanging down so low that it can't spin round, gently heat both sides of the spiral for a few seconds: this drives off the moisture content in the paper and makes it stiff.

SPIRAL

Two more ways to decorate a spiral mobile

Japanese Flying Fish

Materials
Tissue paper
Short piece of wire
Sellotape
All-purpose clear adhesive
Strong thin string or nylon thread
A garden cane or a similar slim stick:
   2 ft. (61 cm.) is a good size if the
   stick is to be held in the hand or
   5–7 ft. (1·5–2 m.) if it is to be stuck
   in the ground
Paints or felt-tip pens

Tools
Pencil
Scissors
Ruler
Needle
Wire cutters

Fish   Fold the tissue paper in half and draw on it the shape of the fish (fig. 1). Cut round this outline, through both layers of the tissue paper, so that you have two identical fish shapes.

   Glue along the dotted lines (fig. 1) and stick the two shapes together. Leave it to dry.

   Paint or crayon a large eye and scale patterns on both sides of the fish.

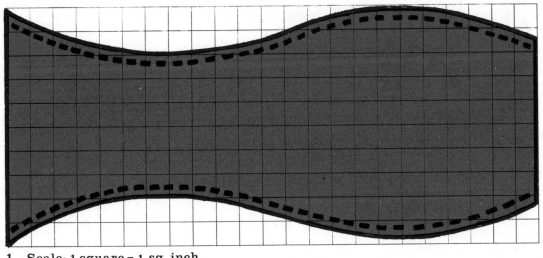

1   Scale: 1 square = 1 sq. inch

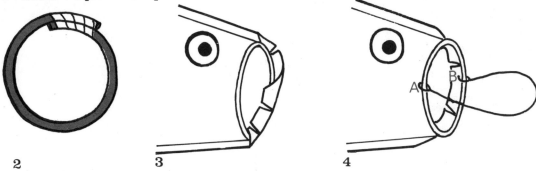

2   3   4

Take a piece of split cane or wire and bind it with Sellotape to form a circle which will fit into the fish's mouth (fig. 2). Insert the circle into the mouth. Glue round the inner edge of the tissue paper opening, fold it over the cane all the way round the circle and press it into position (fig. 3).

Streamers   Cut eight streamers 24 in. (61 cm.) long and glue them in position around the tail (see fish drawing), and then cut four much shorter streamers and glue them around the mouth to look like fish gills.

Attaching the fish to the stick   Thread a needle with a 10 in. (25 cm.) length of strong thread. Pierce the tissue paper at point A (fig. 4) and tie the end of the thread around the cane. Loop the thread over to the other side of the fish head and tie the end of the thread at point B (fig. 4). Attach a length of thread about 24 in. (61 cm.) long from the centre of loop A–B, and tie the other end tightly round the top of the stick (see fish drawing).

The fish looks most spectacular if it is attached to a very long cane stuck in the ground, because the wind fills the body and blows it about so that it appears to be tossing on waves.

13

Humming Bird

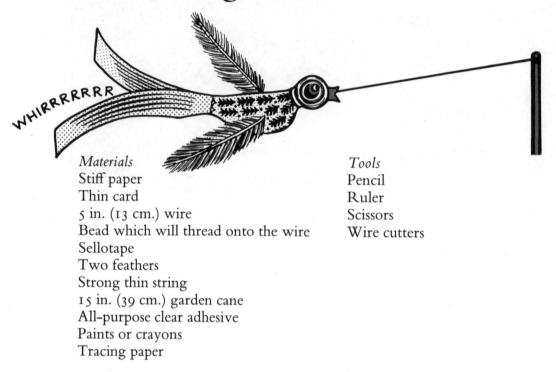

WHIRRRRRRR

Materials
Stiff paper
Thin card
5 in. (13 cm.) wire
Bead which will thread onto the wire
Sellotape
Two feathers
Strong thin string
15 in. (39 cm.) garden cane
All-purpose clear adhesive
Paints or crayons
Tracing paper

Tools
Pencil
Ruler
Scissors
Wire cutters

Fold the paper in half and draw or trace on it the shape of the bird (fig. 1). Cut round the outline through both halves of the paper so that you have two bird shapes. Decorate them with paint, crayons or stuck-on feathers. Cut the slits shown on the body and head. Overlap parts A to parts B and glue them in position.

Draw or trace the tail (fig. 2) onto thin card and cut it out. Pierce the two holes, C and D, indicated. Push the wire into the first hole and out through the second hole. Bend the end of the wire back and press it flat to hold the tail firmly in position (fig. 3). Curve the two pieces of the tail between your thumb and finger to form a Y shape (see bird drawing).

Thread a bead onto the other end of the wire, bending the end, so that the bead can't fall off (fig. 4). Wrap a piece of sellotape round the bead to form a tube (fig. 5) and cut a slit down either side (fig. 6). Cut out a 1 in. (2 cm.) square of card. Pierce a hole in it and tie on a piece of string 3 ft. (90 cm.) long. Attach the card square to the sellotape tube (fig. 7).

Place this tail structure in position inside one bird shape and attach with sellotape (fig. 8). Place the other bird shape on top and stick the two together. Tie the remaining end of string to the top of the garden cane.

To make the wings, pierce a hole either side of the body and push in a feather. Glue if necessary.

When the bird is swung in the air, the tail spins round and makes a whirring sound.

14

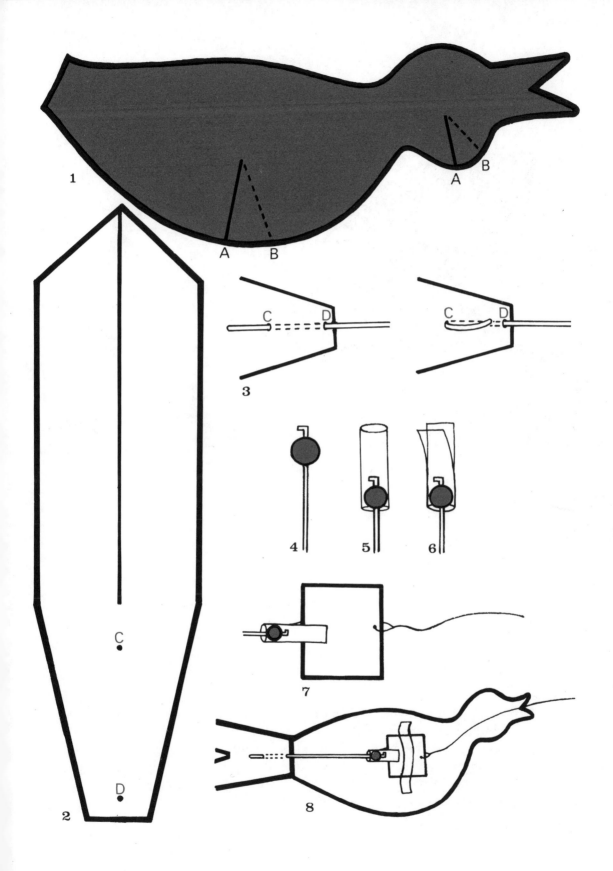

1

2

3

4

5

6

7

8

A B

A B

C D

C D

Kite

Materials
Thin strong paper
32 in. (82 cm.) length of square
    section balsa wood
Strong thread
Ball of thin string
All-purpose clear adhesive
Paints or crayons

Tools
Ruler
Pencil
Scissors

Kite   With a sharp knife, cut the balsa wood into two pieces, 18 in. (47 cm.) and 14 in. (35 cm.) long. Carefully measure and mark the centre of the 14 in. (35 cm.) piece. Mark the 18 in. (47 cm.) piece at a point 5 in. (13 cm.) from one end.

Cross the two lengths at these marked points and lash them firmly with strong thread, binding it crossways (fig. 1). Finish with a smear of glue to stop any slipping.

To complete the framework of the kite, a piece of strong thread must be tied round the ends of the cross to form a diamond shaped outline (fig. 2).

Place the kite framework on the sheet of paper. Allowing an extra 1 in. (3 cm.) all round, draw the shape (fig. 3) and cut it out.

16

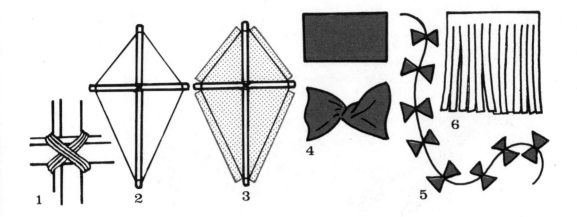

Decorate with paint, crayons, or cut-out paper patterns. Big, bold shapes such as a huge red circle or a thick stripe will look best when the kite is flying high up in the sky.

Glue the flat side of the long stick and 2 in. (5 cm.) at either end of the short stick and place the framework down in position on the paper. Taking each edge of the paper in turn, glue the 1 in. (3 cm.) margin, then fold and stick it down over the thread. Smooth the paper so that it is tight across the framework.

Streamers   Cut out and colour streamers $\frac{1}{2}$ in. (1 cm.) wide and 12 in. (30 cm.) long and glue to the two corners (see kite drawing).

Tail and Boss   A *tail* is necessary to keep the kite upright during flight. Take a piece of string at least 3 yds. (2·75 m.) long. Cut out and colour eight pieces of paper, 4 in. (10 cm.) long by 2 in. (5 cm.) wide. Twist each one in the centre (fig. 4) and tie them equal distances apart along the length of the string (fig. 5).

The bottom of the tail needs a weight, which is called a *boss*. To make the boss, cut a piece of paper 9 in. (23 cm.) by 12 in. (30 cm.). Colour it, and cut into a fringe (fig. 6), roll it into a tassel shape and tie tightly with thread at the top to prevent it unwinding. Tie the boss to the end of the tail. Attach the tail to the bottom end of the kite.

Flying   To complete the kite for flying, tie a piece of string about 24 in. (60 cm.) long from the top to the bottom end of the kite. Then tie your ball of string to this about 10 in. (26 cm.) from the top, as shown in the drawing of the finished kite.

The best kite flying weather is a lovely sunny day with a steadily blowing wind. If the wind is too gusty and strong, the kite will become uncontrollable and could break the string.

17

Two Weather Vanes

Materials
Stiff card
Wire
Bead which will thread onto the wire
Thin bamboo garden cane 2 ft. (60 cm.)
   long for arrow weather vane
Two strong long bamboo garden canes
Paint
All-purpose clear adhesive

Tools
Pencil
Ruler
Scissors and sharp knife
Compass
Pliers with wire cutting attachment

Arrow weather vane   Draw the arrow point and tail onto card and cut them out. Decorate with paint. Make a slit with a sharp knife at either end of the thin bamboo cane. Squeeze some glue into the two slits. Push the point into the slit at one end, and the tail into the slit at the other end, so that an arrow has been made with the bamboo cane forming the shaft. Twist wire round the cane about 5 in. (12·5 cm.) from the tail end (fig. 1) and thread a bead onto the wire.

   Take the thicker bamboo cane and push a compass point down its soft pithy centre at one end to make a channel. Drop the wire attached to the arrow into the channel (fig. 2).

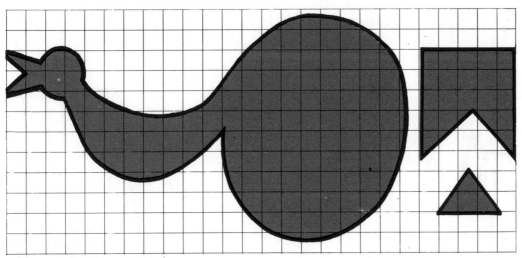

Scale: 1 square = 1 sq. inch

1

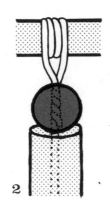

2

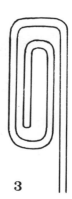

3

Peacock weather vane Draw the peacock shape on to card, cut it out and decorate with paint or cut out paper. Bend wire to make a paper clip shape (fig. 3), slot the peacock into the wire shape and secure it on either side with a blob of glue or piece of sellotape. Thread a bead on the end of the wire shape. Attach the peacock to the bamboo cane using the same method described for the arrow weather vane (fig. 2).

Weather vanes work because they have a big shape at one end and a small shape at the other end. When the wind blows, it pushes against the larger shape making it swing away from the wind's force. This makes the smaller shape, the bird's head or the point of the arrow, move round at the same time to face the direction from which the wind is blowing. If you have a pocket compass you will be able to read where the north, south, east, and west directions are related to the position of the weather vane. These directions can be marked with cardboard pointers stuck onto the bamboo cane. It will then be possible to tell accurately and at a glance, from which direction the wind is blowing at any time of day.

If you want to make a weather vane that will last a long time out of doors, use hardboard instead of card and make it a bit bigger.

19

Simple Mobiles

The mobiles in the next section of this book are indoor decorations hung from thin thread. How do they move without wind or mechanical means? The answer is that when people move through a room, bang doors, open windows or switch on a heater, they create air currents. Air currents are very gentle, and unlike the wind which blows strongly from one direction, they flow in continuous circular patterns all round a room. If a mobile is hung from a thread it will slowly twist, untwist, and swing round as the air currents push against it.

When an indoor mobile is being made, it is a good idea to have somewhere to hang it up easily to test the weight, see what it looks like, and make any alterations. Tie a piece of string, wood or garden cane across the backs of two chairs, then attach the mobile from a bent wire hook. When the mobile is finished, ask your parents or a teacher to help you hang it up. Remember the mobile must not be hung too low or people will keep bumping into it. Three good ways in which to hang mobiles are: from the top of the banisters down into a stair well, from a string or wire stretched between the picture rail on one wall and the picture rail on the opposite wall, or from a string, wire or cane attached at either end to a picture rail, across the corner of a room.

Funny Paper Bag Faces

Materials
Paper bags of any size
Thin string
Old newspapers
All-purpose clear adhesive
Paint, coloured paper, scraps of wool
   and material

Tools
Scissors

Roll up the newspaper into small balls and stuff each paper bag with them until it bulges. Tightly tie the string round the opening, leaving one end of the string very long with which to suspend the bag when it is finished.

Now the faces can be put onto the paper bags using any method you like. They can be painted, drawn with felt-tip pens, or made of cut-out paper and stuck on with glue. Beards, moustaches, hair, and bushy eyebrows can be made of paper streamers curled round a pencil, or from strips of cloth and wool stuck on with glue. The faces can be funny, frightening or sad. They can wear hats or crowns, spectacles, earrings and masks. You could make paper bag heads of all your family using a big paper bag for dad and smaller and smaller ones for the rest of the family.

When the faces are hung from their strings they will swing round in the air current, so you could paint a different face on either side of the same paper bag.

21

Flying Bird

Materials
Card
Paper
All-purpose clear glue
Cotton or thread
Paints or crayons
Tracing paper

Tools
Scissors
Pencil
Ruler.

Draw or trace the outline of the body and tail on to the card. Cut out the two shapes and slots.

Decorate both sides of each shape with paint, crayons, stuck-on paper, real feathers, or by any other method. Don't forget to put a beak and an eye on both sides of the head.

Place the tail shape across the body shape at the slots and push them together. Secure with glue.

Draw or trace two wing shapes onto paper. Cut out and decorate. Gently curve the wing by stroking between your thumb and finger or between your thumb and the edge of a ruler.

Attach the wings to either side of the body (in position shown on body shape) with a dab of glue.

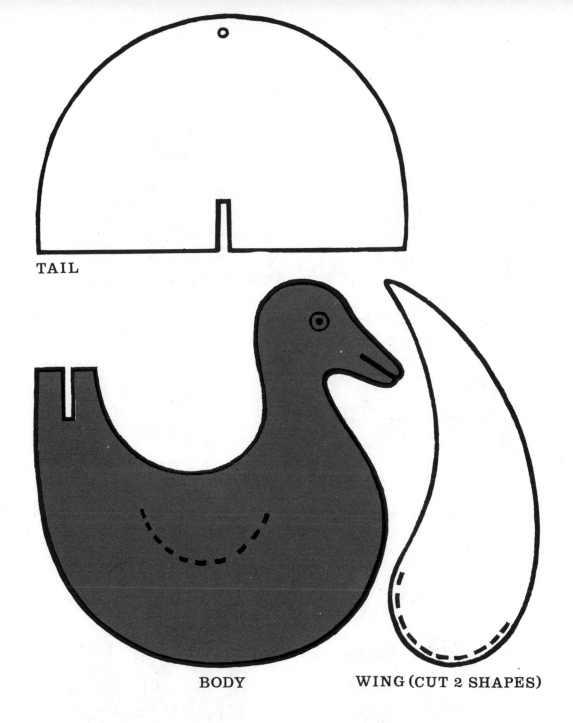

TAIL

BODY

WING (CUT 2 SHAPES)

To make the tail streamers, cut strips of paper $\frac{1}{2}$ in. (1 cm.) wide. Decorate with bright colours. Curl and glue them onto the back of the tail shape.

To hang the bird up, make a hole at the centre top of the tail piece and attach a length of cotton or thread. If it hangs with the head too low add more streamers to the tail to balance it.

Heads, Bodies and Legs

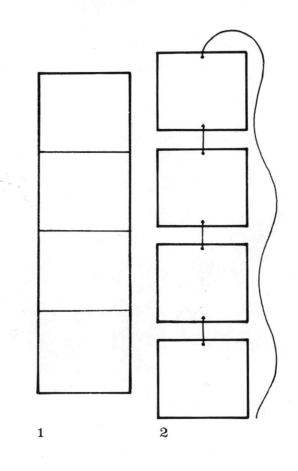

Materials
Card
Thread
Crayons, paints or felt-tip pens

Tools
Ruler
Set square
Pencil
Scissors
Needle

1   2

Cut a strip of card 6 in. (15 cm.) wide, 20 in. (48 cm.) long. With a pencil divide the strip in four 5 in. (12 cm.) rectangles (fig. 1). Now draw a figure on the card. It can be a person or an animal, a fantastic monster, an astronaut, or a beautiful princess. In the top rectangle draw the face and neck, in the second rectangle draw the arms and body down as far as the waist, in the third rectangle draw the legs down to the knees, and in the bottom rectangle draw the rest of the legs and the feet. Turn the card over, divide it into four and draw another figure. Cut the card along the dividing lines into four pieces. Keeping these pieces in the same order, pierce a hole in the centre top and bottom of each piece of card and thread them together again (fig. 2). Tie a long piece of string to the top of the first rectangle and suspend the mobile. When the pieces of card turn in the air currents, the sections of the two figures will become mixed up to form lots of different strange people.

As a variation you could look in old magazines, comics and newspapers for different sorts of heads, bodies, and legs. Cut them out carefully and stick them onto the pieces of card. Or try a mixture of your own drawing and stuck-on pictures, such as two eyes cut out from a magazine stuck onto a drawn face.

Moving Crocodile

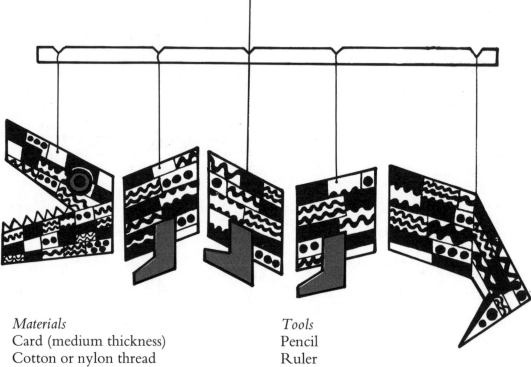

Materials
Card (medium thickness)
Cotton or nylon thread
All-purpose clear adhesive
Paints or scraps of coloured paper for
    collage

Tools
Pencil
Ruler
Set square
Scissors
Sharp knife
Needle

Draw the shapes for the crocodile onto card and cut them out. Stick the legs onto the three centre sections of the crocodile's body. Decorate both sides of each piece of crocodile. Give his body a scaly bumpy sort of texture. This can be done with paint or small scales of paper overlapped and stuck onto the card. Make sure he has a set of sharp gleaming white teeth and wicked looking eyes.

Draw and cut out the support arm of the mobile, 30 in. (76 cm.) long and 1 in. (2·5 cm.) wide.

Pierce the holes shown in the crocodile pieces (see figs.) and tie a length of thread from each one. Arrange the crocodile in its correct order on the floor, allowing a 1 in. (2·5 cm.) space between each piece. Place the support arm above the crocodile and stretch the threads up to it. Now you can see where the threads must tie on to the support arm. Mark the positions with a pencil, cut out a small triangle at each point (see drawing) and attach the threads. The triangular notches will prevent the threads from slipping along the support arm.

26

To hang the mobile up, tie a length of thread from the central triangle of the support arm.

Try making other animal mobiles in the same way. A fish works very well (see drawing), and so does a snake, a dragon or a sea monster.

Scale: 1 square = 1 sq. inch

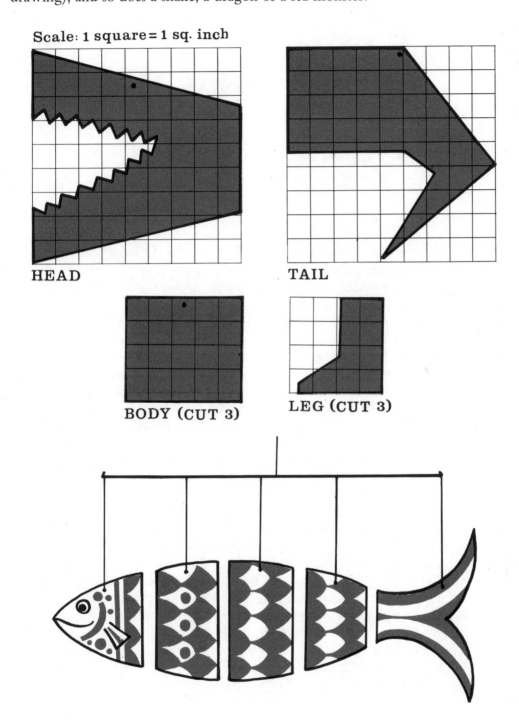

HEAD

TAIL

BODY (CUT 3)

LEG (CUT 3)

Balanced Mobiles

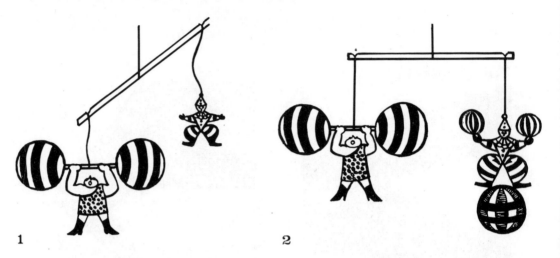

1   2

HOW TO BALANCE A HANGING MOBILE

To make more complicated mobiles which have a lot of different shapes hanging from one bar or from several bars linked together, it is important to understand how to balance the mobile so that it swings round freely without getting the strings tangled in a horrible mess. This is not difficult but it does require some patience.

Look at the circus mobile on the opposite page: there are two figures, one suspended at either end of a horizontal bar which is hanging from a single thread. One of the figures is a little clown; the other is a huge strong man lifting weights. If the piece of thread which is to hang up the mobile is tied to the centre of the bar, the two figures will at once be thrown out of balance, because the strong man is a larger and heavier shape than the clown and will drag his end of the bar down (fig. 1). Perhaps you have seen the same thing happen when two people are sitting on a seesaw. The heavier person will bump down on to the ground and the lighter person will be lifted into the air. If this happens to a mobile there are ways of correcting the balance so that the bar and figures hang evenly.

The place where the string is tied on to the bar to hang up the mobile is called *the point of balance*. The weight on either side of this point must be equal if the two sides are to balance—this means without one end dropping lower than the other, and the support bar hanging in a horizontal position. One way to balance the mobile is to add some extra weight to the light side (fig. 2). The other method is to slide the string very gradually towards the heavier figure, so that the amount of bar and its weight is being decreased on the heavy side and at the same time increased on the lighter side. You will find that at a particular point the weight will become equal on both sides and the mobile will be perfectly balanced. The easiest way to find the correct point of balance is to tie the string in a loose loop round the bar and slide it along until the mobile is evenly balanced. When this point is reached it can be marked with a pencil and the thread tied on tightly at the correct position.

28

Circus

Materials
Thin card
Strip of stiff card 22 in. (56 cm.) long,
   1 in. (2·5 cm.) wide
White or black cotton thread
Crayons, paints, or felt-tip pens

Tools
Small pair of scissors
Sharp knife
Ruler

Draw a clown and a strong man on thin card. Don't make the figures too small—
8 in. (20 cm.) tall is a good size for the clown, and the strong man should be larger,
say, 12 in. (30 cm.) tall. Cut out the two figures and decorate the front and back of
each one with paint, crayons, or felt-tip pens.

    Pierce a small hole with a pin in the top of the clown's hat. Thread a piece of cotton
16 in. (42 cm.) long through the hole and tie one end securely to the clown. Attach
another piece of cotton 16 in. (42 cm.) long to the centre of the strong man's weights.

    Draw and cut out the support bar for the mobile from stiff card, 22 in. (56 cm.)
long, 1 in. (2·5 cm.) wide. Cut out a small triangular notch 1 in. (2·5 cm.) from either
end of the support bar along the top edge.

    Tie the clown to the notch at one end of the support bar, and the strong man to
the notch at the other end, making sure both figures hang down and swing freely.

    To hang up the mobile, find the point of balance on the support bar, as explained
on the opposite page. Firmly tie a length of cotton thread round the support bar
at this point.

Name Mobile

Materials
19 S.W.G. (1 mm.) wire
Thin card
Crayons, paints or felt-tip pens
Nylon or cotton thread
All-purpose clear adhesive

Tools
Pliers/wire cutters
Scissors

Draw all the letters in your name on to thin card. They can be big fat letters, long thin ones, or different sizes jumbled up. Cut them out and decorate both sides of each letter with paint, crayons, or felt-tip pens. Pierce a hole in the top of each letter and attach a thread 10 in. (26 cm.) long.

How many letters are there in your name? Look at the drawing of the mobile and count how many horizontal support bars you will need. For example the name Jane has four letters and will need three support bars, whilst the name Simon has five letters and will need four supports. If you have a very long name hang several letters one under the other from the support bar.

The support bar can be made of stiff card, but wire is stronger and will give the finished mobile a more delicate appearance. Cut each wire support to the required size, then using a pair of pliers bend the ends of the wire to form small hooks from which to suspend the letters (fig. 1).

To construct a mobile with several support bars, always begin at the bottom and make the lowest support bar first. Cut a piece of wire 8 in. (20 cm.) long and bend the ends to form hooks as described above. Suspend a letter from each hook. Tie an 8 in. (20 cm.) length of thread to the centre of the wire and adjust it until the point of balance has been found, then secure it with a small blob of glue.

The second support bar should be slightly longer than the first—9 in. (23 cm.) long. Suspend the first support bar from one hook, and a letter from the other hook. Find the point of balance on the second support bar and attach an 8 in. (20 cm.) length of thread.

Make a third support bar 12 in. (31 cm.) long. Suspend the construction from the hook at one end and a letter from the hook at the other end. If your name has four letters the mobile is now complete. Find the point of balance and attach a thread for hanging up. If your name has five letters you must attach one more support bar 14 in. (36 cm.) long. Suspend the fifth letter from one end, and the construction on the other end. To hang up the mobile, attach a thread to the point of balance on the last support bar.

Design Your Own Mobile

The basic principles and methods of making a hanging mobile with several support bars have been described. Now try experimenting with the different mobile constructions shown in the diagrams. They are all made in exactly the same way as the Circus and Name mobiles. Some of them are very quick and easy to make (fig. 1), whilst others are more complicated (fig. 5) because they have a lot of objects hanging from them and take more time to construct.

For the theme of the mobile, choose a subject which you enjoy—for example football, horses, motor cars, ballet dancing or even monsters! Draw the objects on to thin card and colour them with paint, crayons, or felt-tip pens. Cut the shapes out and decorate them on the other side.

Think what other sorts of material could be stuck on to the objects to make them more decorative. For example, a ballet dancer could have a net or silky material skirt stuck round her waist and sprinkled with glitter or a few sequins. Birds could be decorated with real feathers collected from the garden or park, and stuck on to their tails. A sportsman could have a photograph of his face cut from an old newspaper and stuck on to a painted body. Beads, scraps of material, strands of wool, glitter and silver paper can all be glued to thin card with all-purpose adhesive.

When the objects have been made and you are ready to start putting the mobile together, here are a few points to remember about the construction:

1. To construct a mobile always begin at the bottom and make the lowest support bar first.
2. Support bars and suspension threads must be strong enough to support the decorations. If large, heavy shapes are made, suspend them on nylon thread and use wire support bars.
3. Carefully balance each support bar as it is added to the mobile, by finding the correct point of balance (instructions on page 28).
4. Before the mobile is hung up, make sure that the threads and objects cannot become tangled as the mobile swings round. Adjustments can be made by lengthening or shortening the threads.

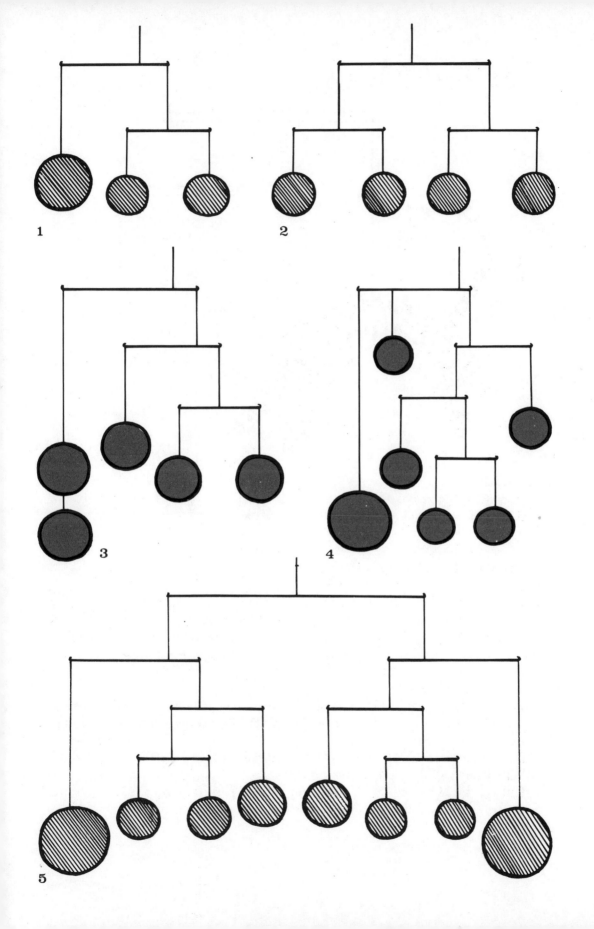

Cat and Mouse

Materials
Thin card, white or coloured
Stiff card or 19 S.W.G. (1 mm.)
   wire for suspension bar
Paint or felt-tip pens
All-purpose clear adhesive

Tools
Pencil
Ruler
Scissors
Sharp knife

Cat   Cut out a piece of thin card, 23 in. (58·5 cm.) long, 5 in. (13 cm.) wide. Draw the outline of the cat on the card (fig. 1), and cut it out.

Place a ruler along the dotted line marked across the top of the cat's head (fig. 1). Run a sharp knife lightly along the ruler edge so that it marks the card, but does not cut through it. The card will then bend crisply and easily along the mark. This is called *scoring* the card.

To make the cat's tail, cut a strip of thin card $24\frac{1}{2}$ in. (63 cm.) long, $1\frac{1}{4}$ in. (3·2 cm.) wide. Fold a $\frac{1}{2}$ in. (1 cm.) tab at one end of the tail, and round off the other end with scissors.

Decorate both sides of the cat's body and tail with spots, stripes and patches of colour. Paint a smiling pussy face on the head.

Cut out six whiskers $5\frac{3}{4}$ in. (14·5 cm.) long, $\frac{1}{4}$ in. (0·5 cm.) wide. Glue three whiskers either side of the cat's face with all-purpose clear adhesive.

34

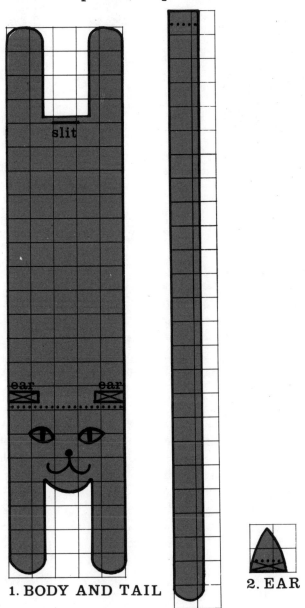

slit

ear   ear

1. BODY AND TAIL   2. EAR

Cut out two pointed ear shapes and fold along the dotted lines to make tabs (fig. 2). Attach the ears to the cat's head by gluing the ear tabs in the position shown (fig. 1).

Make a slit 1¼ in. (3·2 cm.) wide in position shown at the end of the cat's body (fig. 1). Glue the tab at the end of the tail shape, to the inside of the cat's chin. Pull the other end of the tail through the slit in the cat's body, so that the cat's back is

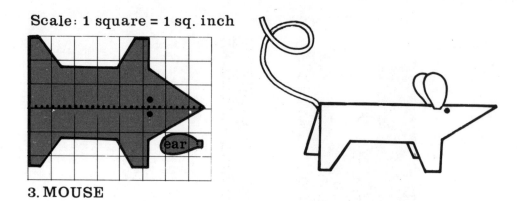

Scale: 1 square = 1 sq. inch

ear

3. MOUSE

arched and a long tail formed. The tail may be held in position with a small blob of glue smeared along the slit. Curve the tail by stroking it gently between your thumb and the edge of a ruler.

Mice   Cut out two pieces of card, $5\frac{1}{2}$ in. (14 cm.) wide, $7\frac{3}{4}$ in. (19·7 cm.) long. Draw the outline of the mouse on each card (fig. 3) and cut them out. Score along the dotted line down the centre of the mouse shapes, and fold in half. Cut out four ears. Glue two ears on to each mouse, positioning them either side of the head. Decorate the mice with felt-tip pens, giving them pink-tipped noses and an eye on either side of the head. Cut out two long thin curly tails and attach to the mice with all-purpose clear adhesive.

To construct the mobile   Find the point of balance on each mouse shape by tying a loop of thread round the body and sliding it along until the mouse is hanging evenly in a horizontal position. Pierce a hole at this point in the fold along the body. Cut two threads, 15 in. (38 cm.) and 13 in. (32·5 cm.) long, knot one end of each. Pull one thread up through the hole in the back of each mouse.
   Cut a suspension bar from stiff card or wire, 13 in. (32·5 cm.) long. Hang a mouse 1 in. (2·5 cm.) from either end of the suspension bar. Cut a piece of thread 7 in. (17·8 cm.) long. Find the point of balance along the suspension bar and tie the thread securely in this position.
   Cut out a second suspension bar 21 in. (52·9 cm.). Tie the bar with the mice on it 1 in. (2·5 cm.) from one end of this second bar.
   Pierce a hole in the centre of the cat's back, knot and thread through a piece of cotton 20 in. (51 cm.) long. Tie the cat to the other end of the second suspension bar.
   Find the point of balance along the suspension bar and tie on a long piece of cotton to hang the mobile.

Cut Paper Decoration

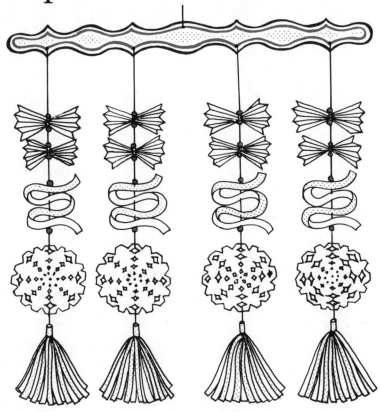

Materials
Stiff paper, white or coloured
Strip of stiff card 24 in. (61 cm.) long,
    2 in. (5 cm.) wide
24 small round beads
Cotton thread
Sellotape
All-purpose clear adhesive

Tools
Scissors
Ruler
Pencil
Needle
Compass

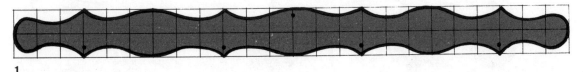

1

Suspension arm   Cut out a strip of stiff card 24 in. (61 cm.) long, 2 in. (5 cm.) wide.
Draw on to it the curved pattern (fig. 1) in pencil and cut round the outline.

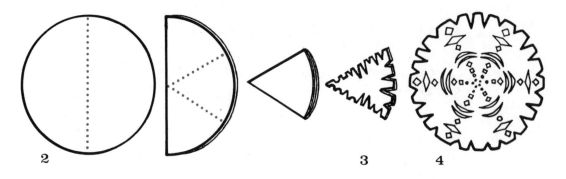

2   3   4

Circle decorations   Draw four circles of radius 2½ in. (6 cm.) with a compass on to stiff paper and cut them out. Fold each circle into six segments (fig. 2). Cut out small diamond shapes down the two folded edges and the outside edge of the circle (fig. 3). Carefully unfold the circle and smooth it flat. It will have become a pretty lacy shape (fig. 4).

Bows   Cut out eight shapes from stiff paper 5½ in. (14 cm.) long, 4½ in. (12·5 cm.) wide. Fold the short end of the paper forwards and backwards to make a pleated effect (fig. 5). Wind a thin strip of Sellotape round the centre of the shape, and pull the edges of the paper out at either side to form a fan shape (fig. 6).

Tassels   Cut out four shapes from stiff paper, 13 in. (33 cm.) long, 4½ in. (12 cm.) wide. Cut along one long edge to form a fine fringe. Roll up tightly into a tassel and secure round the top with sellotape (fig. 7).

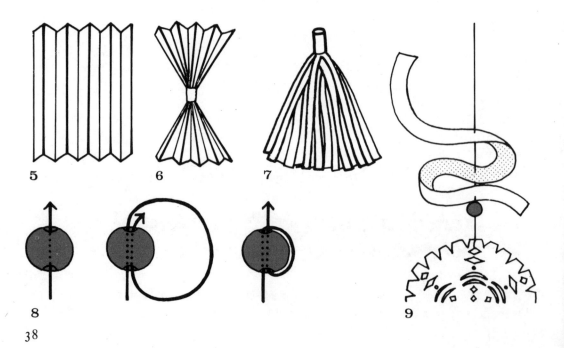

5   6   7

8   9

38

Bent strips of paper   Cut out four strips of stiff paper 37 in. (94 cm.) long, 1 in. (2·5 cm.) wide.

Construction   For this mobile there are to be four lengths of thread hanging from one suspension bar. Each thread has attached to it, one tassel, one circle decoration, one bent strip of paper, two bows, and six beads. To attach the decorations to the threads, repeat the following instructions four times.

Thread a needle with a small amount of cotton and tie a large knot in the end. Push it up through the centre of a tassel so that the tassel is firmly attached and hanging from the end of the cotton.

Push the needle through the edge of a decorative circle, and allowing 1 in. (2·5 cm.) space between the tassel and the circle, tie the thread to the circle. Cut off the loose ends.

Cut a length of cotton 16 in. (14 cm.). Thread it through the top of the circle at a point opposite the hole where the tassel has been attached. Tie one end of the thread securely to the circle.

Loop a bead on to the cotton as shown (fig. 8), 1 in. (2·5 cm.) from the edge of the circle.

Thread a strip of stiff paper on to the cotton. Then bend the strip of paper backwards and forwards, threading it on to the cotton as shown (fig. 9). Loop another bead on top of the paper to keep it in position.

Leave a space of $1\frac{1}{2}$ in. (4 cm.) and loop another bead on to the cotton. Thread on a bow, and then loop on a bead. Leave a $1\frac{1}{2}$ in. (4 cm.) space and attach the second bow between two beads in the same way. Leave a 7 in. (18 cm.) length of cotton to attach to the suspension bar.

Pierce four holes along the suspension bar as shown in the drawing and tie the decorations to these points.

The ends of the suspension bar can be decorated with curled paper streamers. The streamers may be any length and $\frac{1}{2}$ in. (1 cm.) wide. To curl the streamers, stroke them between your thumb and the edge of a ruler, then glue them at each end of the suspension bar with clear all-purpose adhesive.

To hang the mobile, pierce a hole in the centre top of the suspension bar and tie on a long piece of thread.

How to Use Found Objects

1

2

Lots of objects round the house which usually get thrown away have interesting shapes, and can be the basis of all sorts of unusual decorations. Ask your mother whether she has any empty egg boxes, cotton reels, cardboard rolls, plastic containers, straws or other unwanted objects. Make a collection of everything you can find; then spread them out and think what you could make by cutting and gluing them together.

The mobiles in figs. 1 and 2 can be made from any cylinder shape such as cardboard rolls, plastic bottles, cartons or cotton reels. Cut four cylinders so that they vary in size as shown in the drawing. Decorate them with bold patterns or turn them into funny little people. Cut out a circle of card to fit the top of each cylinder. Thread a needle with a length of cotton and tie a large knot in the end. Pull the thread up through the centre of each card circle so that the circle is hanging from the knotted end of the thread. Put strong glue on top edge of cylinders and stick to underside of hanging circles. The cylinders are then hung by the thread on to a wire suspension bar.

Cardboard rolls can usually be cut to different sizes with a sharp pair of scissors. However, if necessary, ask someone older to cut them with a small saw. Decorate the rolls with paint, cut-out paper, scraps of material, and wool. For a shiny effect they can be finished off with a coat of varnish.

Plastic containers can easily be cut with scissors. Cut off the tops of bottles to form cylinder shapes. Wash the containers in warm soapy water. The smooth surface of plastic is difficult to paint, so decorate it with cut-out paper shapes stuck on with all-purpose clear adhesive.

Cotton reels can be stuck on top of one another with all-purpose clear adhesive to form larger shapes. If they are made of plastic, decorate them with enamel paint (obtainable in small tins) or cut-out paper shapes.

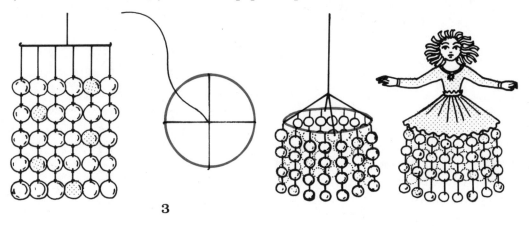

3

Collect as many different coloured milk-bottle tops as possible. Wash them in warm soapy water. When they are dry, press them into flat discs. Make a circle out of wire and hang several threads of bottle tops from it, so that they are just touching or overlapping each other. Tie two pieces of thread across the circle (fig. 3) and attach the suspension thread in the middle. When the mobile moves, the tops will glitter and make a slight tinkling noise as they push against each other. Perhaps you could make the top half of a woman out of thin cardboard and then tie a jingling milk-bottle top skirt to her waist.

Paper drinking straws can be cut and glued together to form a variety of decorative shapes. Work flat on a table. Cut the straws to the size required and stick them together with very small blobs of all-purpose adhesive. Make sure the glue is completely dry before you try to pick up the decoration. To make star shapes it is easier if the straws are flattened out in the centre before they are arranged and glued together.

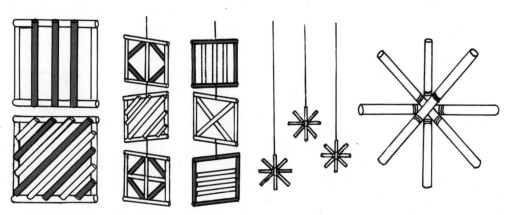

41

How to Make a Cube and Cuboid

It is very convenient to use ready-made objects such as plastic containers and cardboard boxes as starting shapes for mobile decorations, but sometimes it is impossible to find a container that is exactly the right size and shape for the object you would like to make. Therefore it is useful to learn how to make a few simple geometric shapes such as cubes, cuboids, cylinders, and cones.

Cube This is a square box shape. All six sides of a cube are the same size. Draw fig. 1 on to thin card, carefully measuring and drawing the lines with a ruler. Use a set square to make sure that all the angles are ninety degrees. Cut out the shape and score along the dotted lines. Fold into a cube (fig. 2). Smear the tabs with all-purpose clear adhesive and tuck them inside the edges of the cube, pressing lightly to make sure the cube is firmly stuck together.

Cuboid This is an oblong box shape. Four of the sides are long and thin, and the two ends are square. Carefully draw fig. 3 on to thin card using a ruler and set square. Cut the shape out and score along the dotted lines. Fold the card into a cuboid, tucking the tabs inside and sticking them down with all-purpose clear adhesive.

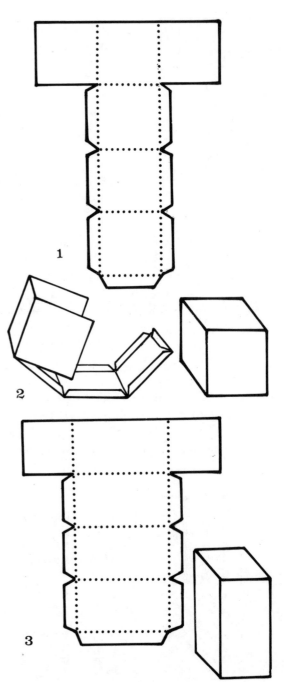

1

2

3

42

How to Make Cylinders and Cones

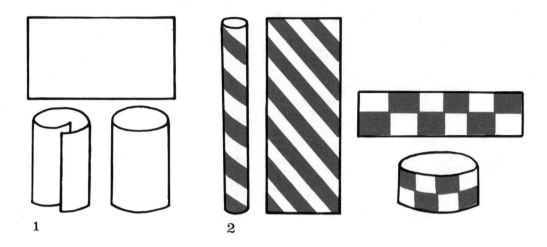

1

2

Cylinders   Cut out an oblong shape from stiff paper or thin card. Roll it into a cylinder (fig. 1), and stick the two overlapping edges together with clear adhesive.

Experiment with different sized cylinders (fig. 2). The shapes can be used to make the mobiles on page 40.

Cones   Using a compass, draw half a circle on a piece of stiff paper or thin card. Join the two ends of the half circle with a straight line. Cut out the shape (fig. 3). Curve the paper by stroking it gently between your thumb and finger, and fold it into a cone shape (fig. 4), sticking the overlapping edges together with clear adhesive.

The shape of the cone can be varied. A long thin cone is made from a quarter circle shape (fig. 5), and a wider flatter cone is made from a complete circle with only a small segment cut from it (fig. 6).

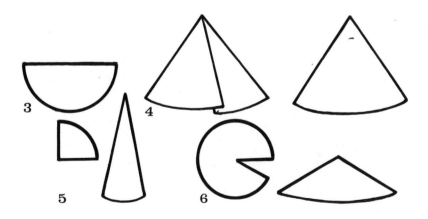

3   4

5   6

Space Mobile

Materials
Thin card
22 in. length of 19 S.W.G. (1 mm.)
 thickness wire
Cotton thread
All-purpose clear adhesive
Paint/felt-tip pens/Christmas glitter

Tools
Compass
Ruler
Scissors
Wire cutters/pliers

Draw and cut out a moon 4 in. (10 cm.) high and a star 3 in. (8 cm.) high from thin card. Paint them on both sides or decorate with metallic paper and Christmas glitter. Pierce a small hole in the top of each shape and tie on a piece of cotton 4 in. (10·2 cm.) long.

Flying Saucer Draw three circles of radius 2 in. (5 cm.) on thin card and cut them out. Cut a small segment from two of the circles (fig. 6, page 43) and make them into cones. Smear the base of each cone with glue and stick one either side of the third remaining circle.

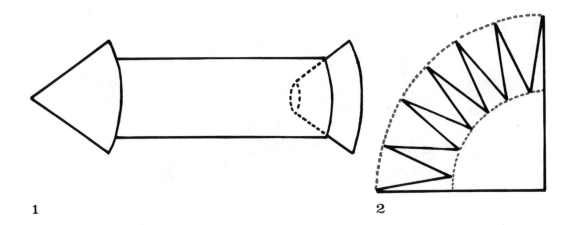

1   2

Pierce a small hole in the top of the flying saucer and push into it a small bent wire hook. Secure the hook with a blob of glue, and tie on a piece of cotton 4 in. (10·2 cm.) long. Paint a row of portholes and a door on the flying saucer.

Rocket   Draw an oblong 6 in. (15·3 cm.) long, $6\frac{1}{2}$ in. (16·5 cm.) wide on thin card. Cut out the shape and make it into a cylinder, overlapping the two edges by $\frac{1}{2}$ in. (1·3 cm.).

Draw two half circles of radius $2\frac{1}{2}$ in. (6·3 cm.). Cut them out and make into cones. Smear glue round one end of the cylinder and push a cone down firmly on top of it. This forms the rocket head.

Cut off the pointed end of the other cone to make a hole approx. $\frac{1}{2}$ in. (1·3 cm.) diameter. Smear glue round the remaining end of the cylinder. Push the narrower end of the cone firmly into the cylinder (fig. 1). This forms the rocket tail.

To look realistic, the rocket must have a jet of flames shooting out of the tail. Draw a quarter circle radius $6\frac{1}{2}$ in. (16·5 cm.) and cut out the shape. Draw and cut out the zig-zag pattern round the curved edge of the shape (fig. 2). Colour it scarlet and make into a cone. Smear glue round the cone point and push it firmly into the hole at the tail end of the rocket.

Paint the rocket. Attach a bent wire hook to its centre and tie on a piece of cotton 7 in. (17·8 cm.) long.

Construction   Cut three suspension bars 8 in. (20·3 cm.) long, 9 in. (23 cm.) long, and 12 in. (31 cm.) long. Follow the instructions for making a hanging mobile given earlier in the book.

Variations   As well as a star and moon, floating spacemen could be drawn, cut out of thin card, and hung from the space rocket or from extra suspension bars. Try designing your own space ships, lunar modules, and flying saucers.

Free-standing Mobile

Materials
Block of wood 6–10 in. (15–26 cm.)
   square, ¾–1 in. (2–3 cm.) deep
Cork from a bottle
All-purpose clear adhesive
36 in. (92 cm.) thick wire, 10 S.W.G.
   (3·15 mm.)
34 in. (87 cm.) thin wire, 19 S.W.G.
   (1 mm.)
7 small fishing tackle swivels
   (available from sports shops)

Tools
Ruler
Pliers
Wire cutters
Compass

This mobile is supported on a strong wood base, and can be placed on any flat surface. A large free-standing mobile looks very exciting in the corner of a room,

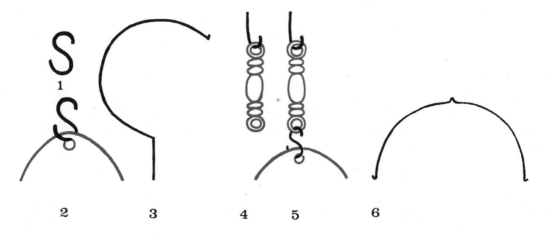

2   3   4   5   6

and small delicate versions of the mobile make very pretty table decorations for Christmas and birthday parties.

You can hang any sort of decoration from the suspension arms, either simple shapes drawn and cut out of thin card, or much heavier objects such as shiny glass Christmas balls. The shape of the mobile structure is similar to a plant or tree, and therefore looks very good with decorative leaves, flowers, and fruit hanging from it, as shown in the drawing.

Construction First of all, decide what sort of decoration you would like to hang from the suspension arms and make four of them. Bend four small S hooks out of thin wire (fig. 1) and attach one to the top of each decoration (fig. 2).

Glue the round end of the cork to the centre of the block of wood with all-purpose clear adhesive. When the glue is dry, push a compass point three-quarters of the way down the centre of the cork to form a deep hole.

Cut a piece of thick wire 36 in. (91.5 cm.) long. Slowly and carefully bend the wire to the shape shown in fig. 3.

Push the straight end of the wire shape down into the cork. If the wire is too loose and wobbles about in the hole, secure it with a blob of all-purpose clear adhesive.

Cut the first suspension arm from thin wire, 11 in. (28 cm.) long. Curve the wire into a U shape (see fig. 6), and bend a small hook at either end. Thread a swivel onto each hook (fig. 4). Attach a decoration to each swivel (fig. 5).

Find the point of balance on the suspension arm, and mark it with a small bend in the wire (fig. 6). Unhook one of the decorations so that it is possible to slide a swivel onto the suspension arm and into position at the point of balance. The little bend in the wire at the point of balance stops the swivel from sliding out of position and unbalancing the mobile. Replace the decoration that was taken off the hook.

Cut the second suspension arm 10 in. (25 cm.) long. Curve it slightly less than the first and bend a hook at either end. Attach the first suspension arm by the swivel at its point of balance to the hook at one end of the second suspension arm. Attach a decoration to the other end.

Find the point of balance on this suspension arm and make a bend in the wire. Remove the decoration from the end of the arm and slide a swivel into position at the point of balance. Replace the decoration.

Cut the third suspension arm 11 in. (28 cm.) long, curve it very slightly and bend a hook at either end. Attach the second suspension arm to one end of the wire, and a decoration to the other end. Find the point of balance and make a bend in the wire. Remove the decoration and position a swivel at the point of balance. Replace the decoration.

Hang the completed mobile, by the swivel at the point of balance on this third suspension arm, to the hook in the end of the curved piece of wire attached to the wooden base.

More Ideas

There is room in this book to describe only the basic principles and techniques required to make mobiles. You will probably think of a lot more ideas and possibilities that haven't even been mentioned.

For example, interesting mobiles can be constructed to make noises when they move. This can be done by adding small bells, wooden clappers, rustling grasses and paper streamers to the decorations. Try making a scarecrow for the garden that can swing round and make a noise to scare off the birds.

There are also exciting possibilities to explore using the effects of bright light on see-through materials such as coloured cellophane or 'Acetate', which is a plastic material that looks like cellophane but is thicker, tougher, and comes in much stronger colours. When decorations are made from these see-through materials and hung in a room, the electric light shines through the shapes and throws moving patches of colour onto the walls and ceiling. Similar effects can be achieved by using reflective materials such as shiny metallic objects and small mirrors suspended on swivels from thin wires.

If you are mechanically minded you might think of ways to create a lot more movement in a mobile, instead of relying on the wind or air currents. A construction could be driven by a very simple electric motor, or attached to the mechanism of an old alarm clock or record turntable.

Other hobbies can be incorporated into mobile making. For example, special skills such as sewing or carpentry are useful to make unusual decorations. A collection of model aircraft or similar light objects can be displayed in your bedroom in a very interesting way by suspending them from a mobile construction.

Experiment as much as possible with new ideas and lots of different materials. Even if your constructions don't always quite work out in the way you imagined, the results will become better all the time!